Mirroring

Mirroring

Selected Poems of
Vladimír Holan

Translated from the Czech by
C. G. Hanzlicek and Dana Hábová

 Wesleyan University Press
Middletown, Connecticut

Czech originals published by Vydal Odeon in the following
editions: *Lamento* (1970); *Příběhy* (1970); *Dokumenty*
(1976); *Sebrané spisy Vladimíra Holana svazek (IV)* (1977);
Propast propasti (1982).

Some of the translations first appeared in *The American
Poetry Review*.

LIBRARY OF CONGRESS CATALOGING IN PUBLICATION DATA
Holan, Vladimír
Mirroring: selected poems of Vladimír Holan.
(Wesleyan poetry in translation)
I. Hanzlicek, C. G., 1942-   . II. Hábová, Dana.
III. Title. IV. Series.
PG5038.H62A24   1985   891.8′615   84-20967
ISBN 0-8195-5129-5 (alk. paper)
ISBN 0-8195-6119-3 (pbk. : alk. paper)

All inquiries and permission requests should be addressed to
the Publisher, Wesleyan University Press, 110 Mt. Vernon
Street, Middletown, Connecticut 06457.

Distributed by Harper & Row Publishers, Keystone Industrial
Park, Scranton, Pennsylvania 18512.

Manufactured in the United States of America

First Edition
Wesleyan Poetry in Translation

Contents

Acknowledgments

Thanks must go to many people for help in this project.

For many years I dreamed idly about bringing the poems of Vladimír Holan to an American audience. It was another fine Czech poet, Miroslav Holub, who first suggested in a conversation about Holan that my ambition might not have to be an idle one. It was he who put me in touch with two people in Prague: Vladimír Justl, Holan's editor, and Dana Hábová, my cotranslator.

Vladimír Justl is a totally devoted editor. I think he knows all of Holan by heart, and he brings great understanding to the poems. His help was crucial in making the selection, since Holan wrote over 30,000 lines of poetry.

Dana Hábová's Czech-English literal versions of the poems were reflections of her knowledge of both languages, and they made my life easy. Without her steady intelligence this project would doubtless have died an early death.

Thanks are also due to Philip Levine for his careful criticisms of the manuscript, and to Peter Everwine for his criticisms and encouragement through thick and thin.

C.G.H.

Mirroring

Introduction

... the poet and artist worthy of the name transforms and re-creates this world, either by the force of humility or by the force of revolt, but always with a singular goal: *to liberate* ... how could this poet, even simply as a man, not desire to smash, once and for all, all that the ruthless bourgeoisie had agreed upon, to smash all its niggardly virtues, its potbellied, possessive feelings, which it made into destiny, spitting on everything that is still miraculous and opens the space for adventure? How could the poet (inside and outside) not long to change the face of this selfish, bestial, catastrophic world, to change it with a singular goal: *to arrive at man at last?* Because millions of us have not become people yet, and I can see only too well those painful mouths, those grim lines of hunger, poverty, and beastly humiliation!

         —Vladimír Holan, May 1946

If ever a life was wholly given to poetry, it was the life of the Czech poet Vladimír Holan, which ended after seventy-five years in 1980. Holan worked in the government Pensions Office from 1927 to 1933 and edited two arts journals from 1933 to 1940. In 1940, he decided to devote all of his time to writing. The poems composed during the war years are filled with antifacist sentiment, and some of those written after the liberation, such as "May, 1945" and "Three of Them," portray the Russian soldier as an almost mythical hero. Ironically, Holan was accused of "decadent formalism" in 1948, and from that year until 1963, his work was officially ignored and little of it was published (the dates given in this volume are dates of composition, not publication). Holan had always been an intensely private man, and he completely retired from social life in 1949, confining himself to the company of his wife and his daughter, who was mentally handicapped and did not speak. Solitude, poverty, and neglect did not deter Holan, and many of his most powerful poems were written while the least attention was being paid to him. Formal recognition came in 1964, when he was given the Award of the Union of Czechoslovak Writers. In 1968, he received his country's highest artistic award: he was named National Artist and Laureate of the State. Other national and international prizes and the translation of his work into eleven languages have led to his being widely considered the greatest of Czech poets. During a writing career that spanned more than fifty years, he produced a body of work astonishing for its size as well as its quality: the collected Holan has been gathered into ten volumes, totaling 3,000 pages.

Because Holan seldom passed a day without making poetry, his poems are a kind of diary of this emotional and intellectual life. The range of subject matter is incredibly broad because he shunned no feeling—whether ecstatic or deeply depressing—and pursued any thought, even if it yielded only a nagging contradiction: "Without death, life is impossible to feel, / with it, life is just thinkable, / and therefore absurd" ("Again?"). Death is a frequent visitor in the poems, and a mocking one at that, and poetry "has only a simile to pit against God's measure" ("Death Comes for the Poet").

Love is in the poems, too. Sometimes it is a reversal that only makes loneliness more apparent—"To be alone is too much for a double, / but being with you I always missed you too"—and sometimes it moves us "as we are moved when listening to a fantasia / composed for two hundred pianos" ("Who Are You?"). Set against the vagaries of romantic love, motherly love is seen as a constant. In "Resurrection" Holan imagines what that event will be like:

> The first one to rise
> will be mother . . . We'll hear her

quietly making the fire,
quietly putting the kettle on,
and cozily taking the coffee grinder out of the cupboard.
We'll be at home again.

In "Visiting Mama after Many Years," he finds that to fall asleep while basking in a mother's love is to become a child again:

. . . you feel well . . . Habit, warmth, bliss, and peace,
familiarity of the breath with something almost as savage
    as paradise,
to be given is also to give,
when you lose yourself:
they deny that you are over forty.
And indeed, if you sob a little at dawn,
it's only because a child never laughs while dreaming,
it always cries . . . A child!

There are many encounters with children in the poems. In "Joy," Holan delights in the manic bliss of a little girl who is allowed to take swimming lessons at an earlier than usual age because she's taller than her peers. This happy poem, however, lies between two poems that chronicle the terrible sufferings of children during the war. Children should be allowed their childhood, adults should be allowed to retain a bit of their innocence, and he cannot forgive "people / who without mercy / forced you to give up the world / in the children's playground" ("Never I").

Holan witnessed too much to hang on to his innocence, but his mind is often playful. As he says in "It Was Raining," "I am all for foolishness." His humor, though, is foolish like a fox. I have noted that sly sense of humor so often in Czechs that I can only conclude it results from an extra chromosome in their genes. The poem "Vision" gives us Holan having fun:

This place, which warned its own remoteness
it would turn into a desert,

still has a few trees left and a few blue tits in them,
calling: thorn-in-the-ass, thorn-in-the-ass, thorn-in-the-ass!

They're calling to the weary or apathetic human being
who is out for a walk holding a book,
and while wondering
what's for supper, he mumbles:
"I've never thought like that or felt like that;
I've never said this!"

Socrates, reading Plato . . .

There are those flashes of the comic, and then we see the
other side of the coin: rage. There is rage against the war, and
rage against the fact that one leaves the war only to come face
to face with the poor and the wretched, ". . . who as adults in
'times of peace' are buried in sugar crates, / and as children
are buried in soapboxes" ("In the Yard of the Policlinic"). One
of Holan's most bitter poems is "To the Enemies," which con-
cerns itself with the difficulties of being a poet and a man in a
world where so many people love no one, not even them-
selves. In this world, "To be is not easy . . . Only shitting is
easy," and it is also a world where science, the hope of many,
has failed:

> . . . To be a poet and a man
> means to be a forest without trees
> and to see . . . A scientist observes.
> Science can only forage for truth:
> forage yes, take wing no!

The way in which Holan's poetry can take wing is, for me,
its most stunning aspect. So often his imagery takes unex-
pected, startling turns. In the poem "Reminiscence II" (Holan
was fond of using the same title for more than one poem), he
and his father are standing in perfect stillness, looking at a
stand of trees, when suddenly a single tree begins to shiver

like a note of music, but without a sound.
You would have said it was light-hearted joy,
the pure spirit of adventure.
But then the tree began to rustle
like silver rustles as it turns black.
Then it began to quiver
like the skirt of a woman touching
a man's clothes while reading a book in the madhouse.
And then the tree began to tremble and shake,
as if it were shaken by someone
gazing into the black-eyed depths of love—
and I felt I was meant to die that very moment . . .

"Don't worry," my father said, "it's an aspen!"
But I remember to this day how he grew pale
when we came back there later,
and saw an empty chair under the tree . . .

The poems modulate between this mysterious, intricate surface and a bare simplicity that results from Holan reminding himself, "You're alone. As few gestures as possible. Nothing for show" ("Snow").

In "Death Comes for the Poet" he says, "a poet's violent heart / beats mainly in little stories." One of his volumes of poetry was titled *Stories*, and indeed a great many of his poems begin as little stories: a chance meeting with a woman in an elevator, street scenes, an encounter in a park. We are not left with only a plot, however. That distinction between observing and seeing made in "To the Enemies" is brought to bear upon the little stories. There is always the thrust toward meaning beyond the surface of events. Sometimes what began as a little story ends as an abstraction. Holan has no fear of abstractions; in fact, he often treats them as old friends. And old friends, after all, can serve us as another pair of eyes; they can help us see ourselves from another vantage point. No matter how abstract he becomes, Holan does not live in a world of ideas alone. Ideas are vehicles for understanding what he most wants to understand: the human heart. To quote again from "Death Comes for the Poet," which is Holan's ultimate exploration of what it means to be a poet:

> knowledge of events means nothing to him,
> science, that cow on stilts, means nothing—
> if knowledge matters, then it's knowledge of the heart,
> he'll exchange large canvases of history
> for a loft window,

and when we look down with Holan from that loft window, we see a world that is baffling, beautiful, painful, and utterly human.

C. G. Hanzlicek

from On the Move: 1943-1948

On the Sidewalk

She's an old woman hawking newspapers;
every day she hobbles to this place . . .
When she's so tired she can't bear it,
she puts down her bundle of Extras,
sits on it and falls asleep . . .
Those who pass by
got used to her and don't see her any more—
and she, mysterious and silent as a sorceress,
makes invisible everything she should offer.

Mirroring

Waking in the night, I saw through the open window
two moons in the sky,
and in terror I said to myself:
This is doomsday.
Suddenly I was so alone
I had no time for solitude
with its aching stomach of childhood.
I was so poor that even time,
which used to hide
in the poems I'd just written
and therefore wished they'd die one day,
didn't insist on its power.

O futility! I was so unprepared,
touching like a will-o'-the-wisp
simple things all across the ages,
as if searching might still be a future,
or maybe just because my silent soliloquy,
obeying the rumble from beneath the earth,
tossed my soul from nothing to nothing . . .

But in a while the wind eased the window shut
and there was only one moon in the sky . . .
Doomsday is yet to come.

The Dead Man's Accusation

I was allowed to return to my people for a little while.
Since it was my home country,
I recognized the place where they rent boats,
and I soon reached the village.
The wind was helping the air get into the weeping
    willow's sleeves.
It was Sunday, my family was sitting in the orchard,
my sister carried milk to the cellar.
I didn't think I could scare them.
But when they didn't believe it was me,
I shouldn't have told them I was alive.
Everything scattered and thinned out
to the cries of violets and pansies,
and before me a cobwebbed landscape crumbled,
garland shrub, moonlight,
and an alarm clock on the cemetery wall.

At the Flea Market in Paris

It was early November. The day was buried
in croaking fog. A bunch of blacks,
desperately dressed in coughing shrouds,
loitered from the ragman's stand
to the stalls of the junk peddlers,
tried on each of the winter coats and raincoats,
and put them back . . . They did so
more like people who can't be bribed than someone
who offers too little;
their poverty was that noble.

They lived taking turns:
either the memory of flea-infested warmth or
    the oblivion of warmth
in a biting place, in which, when no one saw them,
their orphanlike gestures trembled,
and self-torturing laughter relied
on the musical ear of death.

It did so in vain . . . For it all looked
as if each hour without monsters
was the enemy of eternity . . .

Who Are You?

I don't know if women are still called my sweet,
I've never asked you if you are happy,
amazing, you don't care and enter my adoration
without making me lie, be jealous, or prove myself
     worthy of love,
a grafted branch, you press against my sharp misery and
     give your entire self
without making me feel guilty,
you eat and drink with me all my hateful confusions
that you illuminated by seeing simply,
you move me without making me feel better than I am,
as we are moved when listening to a fantasia
composed for two hundred pianos,
free, you liberate, and I cannot want more,
I cannot want more—
and yet there's a torturing anxiety in me,
anxiety about someone I will never know!

To be alone is too much for a double,
but being with you I always missed you too . . .

Death

You drove it from your soul many years ago,
and closed that corner trying to forget it all.
You knew it wasn't in music, so you sang,
you knew it wasn't in silence, so you were silent,
you knew it wasn't in loneliness, so you were alone . . .
But what happened today
to frighten you like someone
who in the night suddenly sees
a beam of light under the door
to the next room
where no one has lived for years?

In a Village Cemetery at the Wall of Suicides

Here, where the cockle kisses the photographs of the dead
and where the tombstone nun has the worn motion
    of marble
in the cackling of geese . . . oh yes, it's right here
that everything confirms that man was not created
but made. Even things are just made.
Man and things made at the advice of the dead!
Things wait. Man guesses.
Things beg. He defends himself.
Things age and survive. He is immortal and
    becomes extinct.
Things are abandoned and he is alone,
and he isn't alone only
when his life turns against him . . .

She Asked You

A young girl asked you: What is poetry?
You wanted to tell her: Among other things, it's the fact that
    you are, oh yes, the fact that you are,
and in my fear and wonder,
which are witnessing a miracle,
I'm painfully jealous of your ripe beauty,
and jealous that I must not kiss you and I must not sleep
    with you,
and that I have nothing, and he who has nothing to give
must sing . . .

But you didn't tell her this, you said nothing
and she didn't hear you singing . . .

Passion Week

Am I really alone again, am I in love too little
and silent too little, do I suffer too little,
and do I think I'm free
because I haven't met my fate?

Don't I understand that one can give only
when he himself never got anything?
Was I really full of those proud colors
that tease the light of nothingness to draw it out?

Even art, when the heart serves the pulses
like a lamp serves a typesetter,
left me for my double,
and is belittling me somewhere, creating so much better
now that my dry husk
is worthy of being trampled.

It's raining outside, it's exactly the time
when a wolf goes after swans,
while from the river with its wet paranoia
echoes the roar of drifting wood,
wood for coffins for every living thing . . .

In the Kitchen

You haven't been here for almost a year . . .
    You were afraid to come in . . .
When you did, the emptiness, once so inviting
but later spurned, grew to hate you,
and now it will not rest unless you repent
your present by your present . . .
Everything in here puts you to shame:
linoleum, firewood, a dried-out fly,
bread mold, the rank vinegar of cracked plaster,
the sorrel of stains and the tan of musty air,
and fretting cobwebs lurking in corners,
and beneath all of it silence, right in that place
where the moon shines only in the daytime . . .
But among all these things you suddenly notice
(with the cruel, very ordinary and very mysterious
finality of a whole lifetime)
a coffee cup with traces of red
where it was touched for the last time
by the lips of the one who left you . . .

Child

The child puts its ear to the rail
and listens to the train . . .
Lost in the omnipresent music
it cares very little
whether the train is coming or going . . .
Only you kept waiting for someone,
kept saying good-bye to someone,
until you found yourself and now you are nowhere . . .

Stay

Stay with me, don't leave me yet,
my future is so empty
only you can help me keep my proud humility
from asking any more questions!

Stay with me, don't leave me yet,
have pity on my impatience,
which, idly written down in a prison ship's log,
is so constant that it almost rivals eternity!

Stay with me, don't leave me yet,
you don't know how to get angry, you never stay angry
    for long,
and where would you go and where would you be
when you got over your feelings? Wait a little, wait,
wait at least until that moment
when the postman comes with letters only for you!

Epoch

We were never quite it. We only resembled it,
but we resembled it completely.
Now, when we begin to be it summarily,
we only shape ourselves to a part of the image
we're going to abandon totally in the future.
What will we become, I wonder? . . .

from For You: 1947-1949

May, 1945

I.

I can still hear it: it was Saturday and the whistles of
    all locomotives
announced to us, the Hopeful from Hopetown,
the departure for freedom from all stations of revolt.
The explosive atmosphere, which for months had been
    carrying and expecting in a corner,
gave birth to cannons and deranged machine guns
that perforated bodies,
so easily severed from souls at the post office of death.
And it didn't take long and Prague with all its torn-up
    paving stones,
sand, puddles, and felled trees
looked as if a new city were about to be founded, the City
    of Extinction.

II.

I'm not going to sing about heroes . . . Their manly being
lies in their silence and in our wordless shame.
But there were children, the same children who for
    several years,
upon hearing the wailing sirens, quickly packed their
    favorite things
into "air raid bags"—
the same children who in May were driven
in front of the German butchers' tanks.
Those and others who had not been slaughtered
    and mutilated,
those who went sobbing from door to door
and at last found their defenseless loved ones,

who still wake up from nightmares and scream:
"Mummy, where's my leg!"

III.
And I saw a man shooting
at a German plane with a popgun . . .
And I saw two trucks passing each other at Smichov:
one carried the dead from Zbraslav
and the other live calves and a large inscription:
    Gift for Prague.
It's insane, what I'm saying, but that's what life was like.

IV.
And I know a painter . . . Knife in hand, he guarded a
    poorhouse.
On the ninth day at dawn he heard a banging on the door.
He opened the door and saw a dust-covered human being
spreading gigantic arms
and in Russian saying, simply and with a smile: "You
    know me!"

V.
And who could ever forget an old man,
who, enraptured, skipped in front of the enormous
    Soviet tanks
and removed every tiny pebble in their way!

June, July, and August, 1945

Do you remember? No! Let me help you:
they were months of scorching heat, ruins, and dust
moistened only in places where women watered flowers
at hastily built little memorials,
but children already played at being barricade fighters and
    generals in bunkers,
and shrilled like the recently silenced alarm sirens,
and yelled loudly that an air raid is reported,
while street loudspeakers called: "Relatives of the missing
should visit the *Collecting Center for Corpses* in such-and-
    such district,
or else the dead will be buried in a common grave!—
It was freedom, yes, it was freedom,
but with all its still murky massive features,
there was some wind here and there, and it blew loathingly,
as if it had found a German hair between two pages of a
    brand-new book,
every large square was sick at heart,
scabby buses from concentration camps arrived there:
"Kadel, my love! . . . Annie! . . . All right, Mary,
stop crying! You're back home, you know? . . . One more,
    one more kiss Jenda!"
I'm telling you, they were months of scorching heat, ruins,
    and dust
moistened only by the tears of the returned ones, the
    welcoming ones,
they all stood there, absolutely free, like at a time
when we don't want anything else,
after a brief sorrowful moment
the memory of the dead began searching in pockets
for tangible keepsakes: a woman's lock of hair,

and a man's red censor's pencil of shame
deleting the carved wrinkles on the face of a tragedy
and transforming it into a smile of self-denial.
They were standing there, in a brotherhood so unanimous
you could hardly grasp that they could return to their
     sentimental homes,
return with the desire to catch up on all the missed
     Christmas Eves,
yes, and when a streetcar moved jerkily,
and some girls grabbed the handrails,
their sleeves pulled up and you could see, just above
     their wrists,
prisoners' tattooed numbers . . .
(They hunted for wide bracelets to cover them,
but it isn't easy to find such a bracelet, my dear!)
And even now, the gates in a Prague street are wide open,
     May-like,
with scribbled words: DO NOT ENTER! SHOOTING GOING ON!
Do you remember? No! I don't want to remember any more,
     either,
but I can still see the splendid Red Army girls,
who at the crossroads of our new destiny
started signaling with their flags
the safe life that's allowed to keep its spontaneity,
the spontaneity of a miracle and love . . .
And I can see a little boy and girl.
She said: "Show me! You got blue teeth?"
But he didn't, he took out another paper bag
and they both dug into more blueberries . . .

Three of Them

I.

He isn't so old . . . But time and again suffering guided the
  sculptor's chisel
and deepened the shallow wrinkles. During the war
he was forced to be a locomotive driver in Germany,
survived several heavy air raids and was wounded
  many times
by Anglo-American bombers hitting the trains' boilers. Since
  that time
his legs have been subject to attacks of paralysis. All
  of a sudden
he falls down and feels ashamed. "Yesterday," he says,
"I had to fork over a hundred crowns, because I fell
into a crate of eggs . . . Believe me, not me, but my destiny
had more irony than it could drink, because with my defect
I got a job in a glass factory,
and I either carry glass or truck it.
I'm pregnant with the fear
that I'll smash the glass on the unforeseeable . . .
But when I carry something heavy, I don't fall,
I usually fall when it's something lighter.
I feel calm enough when I'm fishing in Troja . . .
I also worry about table corners and all edges on furniture.
I tell my wife: Don't stand in front of me!" . . .

II.

The other one, a machine fitter,
went to Holland on German orders.
"I stayed there," he says, "for ages . . .
I remember the Russians best . . . They suffered the most,
nobody here has any idea about that.

They took their shoes off and gave them to Germans
    for a piece of bread.
When we told them they needed the shoes, they said:
'We gotta eat, let's croak later, but
we gotta eat!' . . . That's what I remember best . . .
Yeah, but you should've seen the invasion in Holland,
when the Western Allies
cut the ribbon at last! All those
floating dead, all those flooded villages!
Then the Limeys came, I wanted to go to Russia
or home, but (the war was going on all the time)
they didn't want to let me go, they wanted me
to repair their tanks . . .
When I got to Prague, I had only my overalls,
it was July . . . I've been a driver ever since,
I'm 42, I got no one here,
my mum lives in Moravia . . .''

III.

The third one is a woman. This is her confession: "My
    husband's family
was from the Sudetenland. Mum went crazy
running away from Hitler in '38. Later Dad
got killed in an air raid in Kladno. And their son,
my husband, was tortured to death by Germans during the
    May revolution
at Masaryk's Station; he worked there.
But why do I tell you all this: now they're checking
all pensions for widows of those killed in the revolution,
and I think it's fair, because many of them
have no right to get the pension; you see:

for instance, that woman's husband went to get some beer
and got shot . . . But anyway,
it's terrible when they ask me
what my husband held in his hand when he got killed.
What can I tell them, only that I saw him
a few days after he died, and because of the smell
I could hardly step into the room where he was.
Do you remember that heat? And anyway . . .
we were crazy about each other and ever since
he's gone, I'm always worried
something horrible is about to happen,
worried that he'll suddenly appear in the doorway
(and he did, several times)
as a white ghost in a veil, who takes a deep bow
and leaves . . .

But I still keep in touch with my Joe,
and I couldn't live without him watching over me or
    helping me,
and when I'm chopping wood,
I say: 'How should I split this log, my love,
without hitting the knot?'"

Children at Christmas in 1945

I saw children at Christmas in 1945.
They stood in front of the only stall in Charles Square
and they stood in line. They were pale,
they borrowed shoes from each other and breathed
on the tips of fingers without nails,
but they stood there patiently, humbly, grateful in advance,
awaiting their turn to buy
cotton candy, that sweet air,
because there was nothing else for sale . . .
And I saw a hungry boy running with a briefcase
to get communion wafers at the baker's, looking forward
to eating all the broken pieces at the vicarage.
And I saw a mother who in the morning stuck
tenpenny nails into a sour crab apple
and in the evening gave the apple to her kids,
convinced they would at least get a little iron in
    their blood . . .

World, world, you bastard, what should I do with you?
What should I do with you, if I hear your blackmailing talk
    about
how to safeguard peace so military intervention won't
    become necessary!

Joy

Joy! It exists. It does exist. It really exists!
But if it's only a temptation for us "grownups,"
as incomprehensible as the last words of the dying,
in children it's an excess of still newborn life,
an excess that would like to age a little,
but can't and therefore sings or opens one's heart . . .
So you meet a little girl and it's she who starts wildly,
because she doesn't know how to bear alone
that view into the future, more adult space.
"I," she says, "am three centimeters taller than I should be.
All children sixty centimeters tall *will learn to swim*,
and I'm even three centimeters taller,
so they took me . . ."
She was seven or so, and thin, and kept repeating:
"I'm so happy, I'm so happy!"
and she truly radiated the somehow forgotten essence
and buried lot of our existence.
Then she ran off to other children and told them the
    same news.
But when she came back, she was a little gloomy
and said: "They say that first
I have to have a card, but I knew that
and our teacher trusts me . . ."
And she beamed again, although the malevolent envy
    of her friends
put a few bitter drops into her brightness.
"I don't know when I was born, but I can ask,"
she whispered thoughtfully . . .

The Vltava in 1946

A child is standing on the bank with a heavy bag full of
    windfall plums
and moans and cries because there's no ferryboat.
It's so bestially miserable and so undernourished
that its fingernails haven't begun to grow yet,
and its throat looks as if it were coiled with the rope from a
    death bell . . .
When you take it on the ferry, it says nothing, its distrust is
    immovable,
and only when it unconsciously puts its hand into
    the stream,
it wishes the trip would last longer,
gives you from time to time a resigned glance,
feels like a member of the crew, feels happy,
and suddenly, from this happiness, blurts out:
"I was in a concentration camp . . ."
Come on, don't lie! People refuse to believe . . . "I swear!"
Don't lie! . . . "I swear! I swear!"
says the poor wretch, but no one believes it's true.
So you take it a few times from one bank to the other
and then say good-bye . . . But the child hesitates,
and out of gratitude, as if it wanted to reward you
with something jealously hidden and very precious,
it says: "Mister, we got little rabbits at home!"

In the Yard of the Policlinic

This morning I heard persistent and angry blows on a carpet
beaten in the yard of the policlinic—
and I had to think of all the hearts
persistently and angrily beating
shabby curtains of hope, hope for a kinder future
that wouldn't lie even if it were true.
And I had to think of all those people, people lost
      and begging,
and of those who can't beg, tired as a hand after the war,
I had to think of creatures stuck in the doors of those
who talk while eating and to whom they offered statuettes
      of gargoyles,
threads from virgins' blouses, or ice cream made of
      April snow,
I had to think of those who commune with the fickle grave
      only in the language of whores,
I had to think of all those constantly longing and
      constantly disappointed,
so they know only the anger of desire
and slippery mushrooms instead of May butter,
I had to think of all those *eternally* cheated, so they
      become spiritual,
so spiritual that they are in every body in coughing
      basement apartments
and in every body that hasn't eaten for a long time
and warms its raw hands
at the kitchen fire of imagination with its dipping flames,
I had to think of those desperate men who stumble
in the borrowed shoes of alcohol,
of all those who are so commonplace that they're invisible

in their humiliation, drowned by the goldsmith's
    selfish anvil,
I had to think of all those God could hear about
if children sent him a telegram, if children got hold
    of a radio,
if children weren't as merciless as adults—
I had to think of all those said to be riddles,
who are simply souls nobody feels any mercy for,
I had to think of pale girls in shops in empty passageways,
with lamps lit all day and no customers,
girls who are startled when someone enters to buy a roll,
I had to think of girls who try to hide their pregnancy
and yet produce illegitimate children out of nothingness,
the nothingness of nettles and graveyard plums,
while fate feels like wine
going up into your nose when you laugh,
I had to think of newsboys running beside streetcars
with the wretched servility of tubercular patients and with
    earwigs of cries,
of female singers who lost their voices
and lower their necklines to louden their breasts,
of women servants who, when tidying up the houses
    of the rich,
are only allowed to walk barefoot, on rags thrown
    on the floor,
so they won't dirty the parquet,
I had to think of all those with rings in their noses,
of all those dragged to places where they're needed like salt:
to salt mines, sewers, the sweatshops of Petrak Square,
yes, I had to think of all those, inside whom I am and
    always will be,

as long as there are old forgotten women who
    must beg pitifully
leaning against the railway station wall,
oh yes, there, where people are in such a hurry—
and as long as there are old men, who, though they're just
    the skin and bones of a tombstone epitaph,
have to live and are quickly shut up by dead men's mouths,
oh yes, there, where lazy pedestrians forgot to bring
    their compassion—
and as long as there is poverty and misery,
both apparently disappointed because they're
    misunderstood,
and misunderstood because they're unliberated—
and as long as there are poor people who out of pride
    save up
for a coffin and funeral music—
and as long as there are the wretched ones who are
    down and out,
whose fate boozed up the cashbox at St. Elegy's Church,
and who don't know when they were born or why they
    were named,
and who as adults in "times of peace" are buried in
    sugar crates,
and as children are buried in soapboxes.

from Fear: 1949

To the Enemies

I've had enough of your baseness, and I haven't killed myself
only because I didn't give myself life
and I still love somebody because I love myself.
You may laugh, but only an eagle can attack an eagle
and only Achilles can pity the wounded Hector.
To be is not easy . . . To be a poet and a man
means to be a forest without trees
and to see . . . A scientist observes.
Science can only forage for truth:
forage yes, take wing no! Why?
It's so simple, and I've said it before:
Science is in probability, poetry in parables,
the large cerebral hemisphere
refuses the most exquisite poem by clamoring for sugar . . .
A rooster finds rain repulsive, but that's another story,
it is night, you might say: sexually mature,
and the young lady's breasts are so firm
you could easily break
two glasses of schnapps on them, but that's another story.
And imagine a ship's beacon,
a sailing beacon: but that's an entirely different story.
And your whole development from the stele for man
to the stele of a lichen: but that's an entirely different story!
A cloud is going to vomit, but there's not even a gas leak at
    your place,
you cannot be, you can't even be
strangled by snake scales,
what God conceived, he wants to be felt,
children and drunkards know this,
but they aren't brazen enough to ask

why a mirror fogs when a menstruating woman
    looks into it,
and poets, from love of life, do not ask
why wine moves in the barrels
when she passes by . . .

And I've had enough of your impudence
that permeates everything it wanted to contain
but couldn't embrace.
But a holocaust will come
that you couldn't have dreamed of
having no dreams,
what God conceived, he wants to be felt,
a holocaust will come, children and drunkards know it,
joy could come about only through love,
if love were not passion,
happiness could come about only through love,
if happiness were not passion,
children and drunkards know it . . .
In order to be, you would have to live,
but you won't because you don't live,
and you don't live because you don't love,
because you don't even love yourself, let alone your neighbor.
And I've had enough of your vulgarity,
and I haven't killed myself only because
I didn't give myself life
and I still love somebody because I love myself . . .
You may laugh, but only the female eagle can attack
    the male eagle
and only Briseis the wounded Achilles.
To be is not easy . . . Only shitting is easy . . .

Always

It's not that I don't like living, but life
is so full of lies
that even if I were right,
I'd have to look for truth in death . . .

And that's what I'm doing . . .

Vision

This place, which warned its own remoteness
it would turn into a desert,
still has a few trees left and a few blue tits in them,
calling: thorn-in-the-ass, thorn-in-the-ass, thorn-in-the-ass!

They're calling to the weary or apathetic human being
who is out for a walk holding a book,
and while wondering
what's for supper, he mumbles:
"I've never thought like that or felt like that;
I've never said this!"

Socrates, reading Plato . . .

In the Dance Hall

The humming blackness of her dress, held up by hips,
so filmy that it clings to the body
or flutters around the body . . . To be loved by a virgin!
You poured a glass and handed her respect . . . But she
even refused to touch hands, rightly suspecting
we only promise love from end to end
at both ends . . . Maybe that's the only reason
lovers meet secretly . . .

Here she, the open one, while we conceal our sins,
danced with others, and when the heel of her slipper started
    to wobble,
she left at the very moment you saw
that the flaw in her skirt was in a place
where her crotch wasn't . . .

Only a bad poet hides a snake motif under a flowery
    style . . .

Like Singing

That morning you felt like singing,
and it's possible someone not very close to you
danced to your singing, and, being nice,
danced two or three dances
in spite of your awful lyrics . . .

And the rain in the dill was very nice, too,
and the sparrow was very nice,
still as big as in the days of the pharaohs,
and that man was nice,
who pedaled through the drenched plum-tree alley,
and then jumped off, for no apparent reason,
leaned his bike against the morgue wall, and vanished . . .

But you went on singing: you saw a figure, not an
    apparition,
it was an illusion, not a vision,
in the deep foreground everything was human,
there was no need to fill in some missing thing,
let alone to (as they say) fulfill your fate.

And yet, in a moment like that,
when singing becomes the very fullness of the fullness of life,
we learn, suddenly, that our first love
got married . . .

And Yet . . .

And yet another memory, although I'm saying
  good night to you . . .
About an hour ago, before hearing the news
about the Sarajevo assassination—
I was sitting, a boy, with my father and mother
in a garden restaurant, that is: under chestnut trees.
The heat was intense, washed down with beer,
and maybe a band was playing, I can't remember . . .
I'll never forget, though, how an aged man
came to our table, accompanied
by a ten-year-old boy . . .
I wasn't any older than the boy . . .
But I can still see that man, who
had a snake coiled around his neck,
a stuffed boa constrictor,
and the man displayed the boa for a gulp of beer
or for money . . . I can still see his eyes
and trembling hands, and sawdust
spilling out of the snake. And I can see
the boy picking up the small change,
so that as soon
as his father turned his back for a drink,
he could throw a coin into his mouth . . .

Good night . . .

from Pain: 1949-1954

.

Visiting Mama after Many Years

It's that moment when the fire in the hearth
must be covered with ashes . . .
The hands of your old mother will do it,
the hands that tremble, but the hands that
though trembling still grant
assurance . . . Soothed by them, you fall asleep
and you feel well . . . Habit, warmth, bliss, and peace,
familiarity of the breath with something almost as
    savage as paradise,
to be given is also to give,
when you lose yourself:
they deny that you are over forty.
And indeed, if you sob a little at dawn,
it's only because a child never laughs while dreaming,
it always cries . . . A child!

Dawn

It's the moment when a priest goes to serve mass
on the devil's back.

It's the moment when the heavy suitcase of dawn
uses our spine for a zipper.

It's the moment when it's freezing and there's no sun,
yet the tombstone is warm,
because it's moving.

It's the moment when a lake freezes from the shore,
and man from the heart.

It's the moment when dreams are mere
flea bites on the skin of Marsyas.

It's the moment when trees, wounded by a doe,
are waiting for her to lick the resin.

It's the moment when fragments of clockwork words
are collected by the cunt of the astronomical clock.

It's the moment when only someone's love
dares to descend into the stalagmite cave of tears,
which were secretly suppressed and secretly ate away
    the rock.

It's the moment when you must write a poem
and say it all differently, quite differently . . .

It Is Not

It is not safe where we are at this moment.
Some stars are dangerously approaching
each other. And down here, too,
lovers are forcibly parted
so that time can be accelerated
by their heartbeats.

Only simple people aren't looking for happiness . . .

Meeting in an Elevator

Only the two of us entered the elevator.
We looked at each other and thought of nothing else.
Two lives, a moment, completion, beatitude . . .
She got off on the fifth floor and I, who went further,
knew that I would never see her again,
that this meeting was once in a lifetime and never again,
that even if I followed her, it would be as a dead man,
and that even if she came back to me,
she would come from the other world.

Snow

The snow began to fall at midnight. And it's true
that the best place to sit is in the kitchen,
even if it's the kitchen of insomnia.
It's warm there, you fix some food, drink wine
and look out the window into the familiar eternity.
Why should you worry whether birth and death are only
    two points,
when life is not a straight line after all.
Why should you torture yourself staring at the calendar
and wondering how much is at stake.
And why should you admit you have no money
to buy Saskia a pair of slippers?
And why should you boast
that you suffer more than others.

Even if there were no silence on earth,
that snow would have dreamed it up.
You're alone. As few gestures as possible. Nothing for show.

Reminiscence II

for František Tichý

After hours of crisscrossing the woods
in a vain search for pimpernel, we walked out
at high noon and paused in the heather.
The air was a scorched sheet of metal. We gazed
at the opposite slope with its thick cover
of trees and bushes. They were as still as we were.
I was just about to ask something,
when in that motionless, fixed mass,
so enchanted the spine tingled, a single tree,
in a single spot,
suddenly began to shiver
like a note of music, but without a sound.
You would have said it was light-hearted joy,
the pure spirit of adventure.
But then the tree began to rustle
like silver rustles as it turns black.
Then it began to quiver
like the skirt of a woman touching
a man's clothes while reading a book in the madhouse.
And then the tree began to tremble and shake,
as if it were shaken by someone
gazing into the black-eyed depths of love—
and I felt I was meant to die that very moment . . .

"Don't worry," my father said, "it's an aspen!"
But I remember to this day how he grew pale
when we came back there later,
and saw an empty chair under the tree . . .

After St. Martin's Day II

It was some time after St. Martin's Day . . .
I was walking through the Gahatagat
plain . . . I felt so strange
that I didn't even know what day it was . . .
But the snow had been falling for a long time . . .
    There were deep drifts. . .
And the wind blew so hard
that I lowered my face
and suddenly saw with a shrinking heart
that every step ahead of me
there was a fresh footprint . . .

There wasn't a soul around . . .
Who was it then walking ahead of me?
It was me walking ahead of myself . . .

Resurrection

After this life here, we're to be awakened one day
by the terrible screams of trumpets and bugles?
Forgive me, Lord, but I trust
that the beginning and the resurrection of us, the dead,
will be announced by the crowing of a rooster . . .

We'll lie on for a little longer . . .
The first one to rise
will be mother . . . We'll hear her
quietly making the fire,
quietly putting the kettle on,
and cozily taking the coffee grinder out of the cupboard.
We'll be at home again.

Glimpsed

Glimpsed from an express train that takes
   a shadow for truth . . .
But she was truly beautiful
and she was bareheaded,
she was bareheaded, as if an angel
forgot a head there
and went off with the little hat . . .

from Stories: 1949-1952

Good-Bye

Come, little story, out of this chamber,
where just as our hearing began to decompose a little,
the bluebottle fly of music buzzed in—
come with me into the night and remember with me,
you, who knows that art can't be a mere approximate
    record.

It happened in August on a bench in a park.
The wind bent tree branches as if wishing to build a ship.
A five-year-old girl sat down next to me
and took a book from her bag . . . I asked
if it was a picture book . . . Opening it, she said:
"Oh no, but look here: these children's words!"
Then she ran away and played with a boy.
He shouted: "Stay!" but she ran on.
When he caught her, he urged: "Whoa, oaf!"
And she said: "Whoa, little horse!" After a while
the boy complained he was hungry.
When she offered him a slice of pie, he said longingly:
"When you're hungry, there's nothing like a frankfurter
    and bread."

For these children and for others, an old man used to stand
on the embankment. There was nothing odd about him,
    his face was even shaved,
but the wind around him was so sharp
it beheaded flies with its beard . . . The old man
wavered and in both hands held
about two dozen tiny parasols, artfully made
from wooden skewers and gracefully printed paper
(the Queen of Sheba's whole Dreambook was used up).

The old man tenderly held the parasols
and you beheld one of those defenseless creatures
to whom Fate, pissing through its mouth, says before they
    are born:
"When you crawl from your mother, if you see a carpet,
    come out!
If you don't see a carpet, don't come out!"
The old man held the parasols almost menacingly,
they were the final meaning in his life,
when there was some hope in life . . . He hadn't sold
    a single one . . .
The old man didn't really hold the parasols,
he embraced them, caressed them, dreamed them up,
they were his idea and his endless patience,
his hands trembling. He worked on them
only during the day, when light is almost free,
while at night he would have needed a big tallow candle
with a belfry rope for a wick,
he dreamed them up and could stand proudly with them
like a man from ancient times who rules the present!
The parasols were heavy as words whispered by priests,
the parasols were light as the absolution of sins at
    confession,
the parasols were for children and he loved children,
he couldn't even sell them, he could only give them away . . .

But suddenly the wind blew hard and crushed the old man's
    fragile dream . . .
I can still see him looking at the devastation
and dementedly whispering: "What's my duty in life?"
I can still see him sweeping the remains on the sidewalk

and crumbling them beneath his feet . . . His grief almost
    drove him insane.
He was a sad sight, but he had a militant look. Anger,
when it's suddenly stripped naked and is therefore
    somewhat weakened,
throws a lion's skin over its shoulder . . . But in a moment,
although as a person who can only act from a
    troubled mind,
he took a few steps forward and leaned on the balustrade.

He glanced at the shoulders of the bridge,
painfully proving how the iron constricted their arms,
and then, at his own peril, he looked into the river.

Suddenly he remembered how at the funeral
of the President of the Animal Rescue League,
about fifty dogs stood at attention in front of the
    crematorium,
and a few bulldogs had gold fillings
in their teeth . . . And he remembered a certain Luna
and wondered if he dared to call her Dear, since his buddy
    from the railway station
called his wife Dear . . . And he remembered how he hated
    to go to the cemetery,
but that least favorite path might lead to a chamber
where we'll feel well . . . And he remembered
he was wearing clothes made from his great-grandmother's
    suit,
and if you dreamed about the dead, it would rain . . .
The worst clouds, the best rain, good water, parasols! . . .
Parasols, Luna, dogs, the hook used to pull in

docking boats or drowned men! . . .
And as if from a cloud, but really from a swoon, he heard
the voice of a girl passing by:
"I never dye my hair, I just get a rinse!"
"Yes," he said to himself, "hair rinse, waves, sailing races,
   T-shirts, water, parasols! . . .
Water yes, sun no, water yes, sun no,
water, waves, water, good, good water!"

And he was on the verge of bending forward to it . . . But he
   didn't
until later that night.

Ode to Joy

A sweet summery early evening . . . Summery, because
  summery,
and absurd, because sweet . . . Everything is light
and everything is elevated and the elephants' dance is the
  most elevated . . .

A tear falls in my heart, knowing so well
that the sea is bigger than the earth,
but very deep in my heart the long-forgotten,
half-a-century-dead, simple girl, a maid,
suddenly comes to life . . .

She was twenty then . . . An orphan-virgin,
an archetype of life, but so lacking a model
that not even Fate knew how to earn her love . . .
Because of the laziness of her contemporaries we don't know
  the color of her eyes,
but because of the impatience of her contemporaries I feel
those eyes were trusting and appeasing.
And she was beautiful . . . It was an artless beauty,
beauty that would be mute
had it not once sung in paradise . . .
But she sang and her singing was so much in the present
that even a fragment of a memory
would have violated such innocence.
She was simply happy, and expecting nothing,
she gave her joy to others
and so could never meet herself . . .

She was rarely seen . . . So it's only natural
that men were constantly on the lookout from their
   lighthouse.
Anybody could see her . . . So it's only natural
that women slandered her between her thighs.
Then some boy, blinded by the golden seal of her virginity,
proved that even from divine madness
you can commit a mortal sin, and he killed himself.
Ball-cutting women were offended. Everyone else,
those with glass noses, transparent to show the snot
   and hair,
got mad . . . Lucy ("that whore who has never been
sick") had to leave the district,
where even the veins in the ivy were swollen with
   indignation . . .

I can see her in G. . . . She did some sewing in houses,
   those houses
where the hunting horn doesn't know how to express
its annoyance at plaster columns,
and every Saturday afternoon she cleaned
the office of the local brewery.
She liked the work and did it humbly and silently,
because she honored a secret—
and I don't really know
why a word, a stanza, and a book are born,
or a snake's language from a dog's hand . . .

A sweet Saturday early evening. Saturday, because Saturday,
and absurd, because sweet . . . Everything was light

and everything was elevated and the elephants' dance
      was the most elevated . . .
Lucy entered the office, opened the windows,
and before soaking the rag, she noticed
the Epiphany sign on the door . . .

How (as she stood there) beautiful she was! It was an
      artless beauty,
beauty that would be mute
had it not once sung in paradise . . .
But she sang and her singing was so much in the present
that even a fragment of a memory
would have violated such innocence.
She was simply happy and gave out joy
and so could never meet herself—
and longing for a human being (as a miracle itself does),
she went back to the window and looked outside.

It was St. Wenceslas's Day . . . She saw meadow saffron,
behind the meadow saffron the field eaten into by
      the brick kiln,
and then the alley from which some boys
blew kisses to her . . . But this time she didn't smile
and thought of St. Wenceslas's army
that ages ago passed through this place all night
in brocade skirts, and how
thanks to the Duke's wisdom, there was no battle . . .
Maybe that's why we've been celebrating Christmas
      ever since,
she thought, and suddenly saw her mother

emptying a paper bag of raisins onto the kitchen table . . .
She instantly felt like a child, therefore immortal,
she was nine again, there are nine angels' choirs,
she still enjoyed singing to the smell of Christmas
    raisin bread
and knew nothing about the sex of Luna,
which was painfully opening like the mouth of a gutted
    Christmas carp . . .
Sex? Yes! Several of the boys called to her now,
but her hand was too heavy
to throw her tiny wreath on a tree—
and too light
to draw a lover's face from a hole cut in the ice . . . *

This seamstress, used to holding a bunch of pins between
    her teeth,
unconsciously touched her lips now,
stepped back from the window and went about her work.
Fate, which didn't know how to earn her love,
pushed her head to the floor, and with her pails of pure
    water,
flowing from the fairy-tale Symplegad Mountains,
she scrubbed and wiped the floor with the wig of a
    fallen angel . . .

But suddenly it got dark, so unexpectedly dark,
as if a cloud would be punished for the sin of letting through
    the littlest ray of light . . .

*Translators' note: It was a folk custom for a young girl to peer through a hole in the
ice in order to see the face of her future husband.

She stood up, lit an oil lamp,
and then scrubbed from the corners to the center . . .
In that scrubbing, there was something of a saw
that wants to cut boards for a kinder floor.
In that scrubbing, there was something of a weaver's shuttle
that would weave a carpet for the feet of Jesus Christ.
In that scrubbing, there was something from the height of
    Chaldean astrology,
thrust down to the two stars of her knees.
In that scrubbing, the word and love were looking for
    each other,
and when they found each other, there was silence . . .

Either a hairy bluebottle suddenly buzzed
in front of her eyes,
or a lock of hair tickled her face:
Lucy swung her scrub brush about
and hit the lamp above. She broke it
and the drops of blazing oil
swarmed on her sweaty back like insects before a storm . . .
And she burned and cried . . . And died two days later.

It Was Raining

When it rains, they say a drunk is dying,
and the rooster doesn't crow because he detests the rain . . .

It was raining . . . The light, withdrawn by the left hand of
   the park,
was lying on subjective greenery.
In the wet interval, music,
forced by inches into a soliloquy,
dared to invite an opponent . . .
And he didn't hesitate to leave the funeral procession
   of moments
and sit down at the open fire,
where Venus vulgivaga, the promiscuous Venus, the mother
   of blind love,
closed his eyelids and mine
and opened the conversation . . .

I.

That's not true! I said . . . But he said: It is!
For if love also means caring,
then the indifference of lovers
seems guileless . . . I knew them both . . .
It's not without fear I tell you that they were in love,
learned together, and were to marry shortly,
with a nine-layer cake on a wooden slab
and meat in the parson's fireplace . . .
One day they decided
to go to a fair on the next Sunday,
each to a different village . . . And they would meet
at midnight at the slate quarry . . .

And they met: she, in twenty layers of petticoat,
she, still skilled
at reading musicians' scores,
with a dancing mask fixed on her face
and no longer afraid of snakes . . .
And he, with a few gulps of gin
from Solomon's bottle,
he, the lanky fellow used to leaning his ladder against
    the world
and maybe with his finger beckoning fate in leaden shoes
(because there is always one child who becomes the mother's
    darling!).
One can still see in the moon's lecherous etching how
    they kissed,
held each other in the littlest squeaking door of nature,
and (although now man dies like a dog and only the horse
    and the bee
still pass away) they almost hit the bull's-eye
when suddenly they realized
they hadn't brought any presents for each other from
    the fair . . .

As if all of a sudden they'd found their real names
but couldn't pronounce them,
they were ashamed of their silence for a second,
then stopped looking into each other's eyes with tears hung
    on a nail
from which self-pity and anger later fell down,
and then the reproaches began:
that the other one hadn't even brought a dream,

that after the ancestors there was nothing left,
that they hadn't anything to tell each other,
so they would part as fire above
and water below . . . The old sterile boy, the new barren girl!

They said good-bye . . . They wrote to each other
but threw the unopened letters into the fire,
and the letters sizzled like pig's bile
cast onto embers . . . They never met again . . .

In a quarry, is one piece of stone like another?

II.
That's not true! he said. But I said: It is!
In every month, there is one unlucky day . . .
I once stood on a heath
and saw an abandoned brick kiln . . .
The kiln and the adjacent house
had fallen to decay
from the hangman's hand . . . A shallow ditch surrounded
the bowed walls and caved-in roof.
But windows and a door survived in one wall.
And the door, as I was watching,
suddenly opened, and in it
appeared a woman, a beautiful woman, beautiful
to the point of indignation, amazement, joy
    or foolishness . . .
I am all for foolishness, I was struck dumb and wasn't
    ashamed of my silence . . .
Even if I'd arrived by the latest night train

and had overtaken the sunrise on foot,
I would have missed her dawn . . . Even if I had
fish bile, I couldn't cure my blindness.
Even if I had both banks for a river,
I wouldn't be able to find the spring to feed it.
Even if I'd idolized her,
I wouldn't be allowed to recognize her,
not even by her familiar walk . . .

But she was only *standing*, looking around,
and when she saw that storks were flying to the mountains,
she went back inside
and closed the door . . .

And I, still amazed, was full of desire—
and therefore jealousy—and as if I were to transform
the door of her vanished beauty into the window of
    an asylum
from which I could freely and sadly long
for three worlds, I made my choice,
rushed to the door without a second thought and opened it
and looked behind it . . .

But I found no one.

Perhaps only dust could give shape
to the statue by a sculptor who could re-create her image.
Perhaps only a chimera could bring in a poet,
who, forgetting himself, would be invited by a dream
to materialize her body.

But only Jesus Christ could have
painted the wife of Pontius Pilate there . . .
Only . . . But who knows? . . .

Who knows? Perhaps purity can only be found
   in a desert . . .

Death Comes for the Poet

As soon as he was born, the decision was made . . .
And the one who made it felt joy.
A child like that, in all its being,
can live only by freedom
and for freedom. You might say:
by joy for pain that you can't measure.

Already as a boy he played hooky,
never knew what day it was,
there was always some adventure lurking behind his
    barbarisms,
and on every wooden fence he scrawled
notices in capital letters: DANCING HERE—COME
    ON IN,
and those who read them wanted to become children again
and believe in a future after death . . .
It was his laughter, like Dionysus,
who always came bouncing along on a donkey . . .
But since he can never say, to anything: what do I care!
and since in poetry you're never allowed to dispense with
    anything,
don't ask him to do his duty.
Even if he were a telegrapher, he'd go out
at the moment some "important" news arrived,
and you, indignant, would see him
walking arm in arm with two girls,
you can't understand that, few of you drank,
even once, straight from the spring.

Loyal to the fickleness of life,
he never stays anywhere, the ground always trembles under
    his feet.
It doesn't mean he despises you,
but he's like a flame:
warms you by fleeing from you.

Anyway, if throughout the year most people
can only be seen on All Souls' Day,
he loves his country and the dead so steadily
that the living can't see him,
the living, who take him to be a name
that needs nothing
(il est né aveugle, poète), as indispensably blind as Thamyris,
who was vanquished by the Muses and blinded,
as indispensably blind as Stesichoros, blinded because he
    insulted Helen—
the living, who put on the graves of the dead
a vase emptied of flowers, not a vase that will hold flowers.

It doesn't mean he wouldn't care about you,
wouldn't care about your dread of the suffering
he runs into all the time . . . There may be hairs even
    in your soul,
but he always suffered for other souls
and sometimes speaks for them,
he, who should always come out of himself, and yet
    should love,
he, who isn't always present.

At the stroke of midnight he begins to live
all across the astronomical clock . . . Don't be angry
     with him,
he's awake at night because you're asleep and Jesus Christ
was born at night . . . Who would sing carols for treats,
     let's say,
at the door of a whorehouse? And who would beg
to have their debts forgiven by those
who wouldn't even lend money for diapers?
And who would sin in those hours
when you are beneath the world and only sigh heavily
     above it?
And who would, in heart, spirit, and soul,
accept the dreams you refused in your sleep,
and who would open the door to a postman who only
     comes at night?

And don't be angry with him because his night
is longer than yours: he's delayed a little
by toning down the clock dulcimer with his hand
so it won't wake you up,
or he spends the night with a mother
in the funeral chapel of the little heart to be baptized the
     next day,
for there are children meant for death, baptized in advance,
and there are grownups to be baptized who will die first.

And don't be angry with him because he ran away from the
     wedding

to celebrate the beauty of all women. There's nothing
   he can defend,
only Icarus's bone breaks, but he won't show them . . .
His selfishness takes as its measure
a loneliness more cruel than his poverty,
O you, who have no faith and won't give on credit,
O you, who would like to force him
to scribble on the walls of hell and exalt misery,
when he is here for poverty, pain, sympathy, and the
   celebration of all women
(as indispensably as Orpheus was torn apart by Thracian
   women)—
O woman I saw leaving the house of Lazarus
for the first time, O yes, I understood
that only when supporting ourselves on the ground can
   we get dizzy,
but the beauty of a woman confides only in the melancholy
   of a man.

But a little later I saw you
in the large hall of the Bezdez Castle,
when a few bottles of white wine were lowered in a basket
into the well to be quickly chilled for the king.
But at dusk the jealous king sneaked up behind you,
unsuspecting, covered your eyes with his palms,
and you said: "My dear!" and my name.
Within an hour I was in chains and was soon hanged,
as if the beauty of a woman could confide only in the death
   of a man . . .

Another time I saw you in the kitchen at dawn
making steaks (spreading suet
on the hind parts of a lamb) and celery salad for guests
who didn't feel like going home,
you had to be tired, but no,
such joy was shining out of all your gestures
that I said to myself: the beauty of a woman is beauty only
when it makes a man feel secure. And I thought of mother.

Another time I saw you in all my dreams and omens,
    bursting like pods,
it was my bawdiness that wanted to have you,
I started drinking when I got up
and learned to be silent with a bottle of wine,
as if I'd killed someone,
I hid in the vulval cottage pour voir Carmen
and waited for friends to come and see me,
but they didn't, because I hadn't killed her,
oh, I discovered what lips were and the nether mouth,
and what a bottle of brandy knocked over by a word was,
and a bottle of soda water, gently bubbling,
while people were already up and sweeping sidewalks by
    closed windows,
I discovered what a woman's compassion was, because to
    have her
doesn't mean to know her . . .

Maybe that's why Menandros
visited Aegina for orgies
and Isthmus for mysteries . . . But I

saw you again quite recently:
no pale blue Venus's vein,
but you . . . When you put the baby to bed,
you said: "So you're back again? It's nice of you, and
    don't worry!"
I started crying, because I saw she was no longer beautiful,
but she was patient and humble,
and only because of this patience and humility
can I still sing about beauty, the beauty of a sister of mercy,
about self-sacrifice, about her greatness and man's
    melancholy . . .

And don't say a poet exaggerates everything,
in childhood everything was bigger
and truth is as big as God!—
O you, who have no faith and won't give on credit,
O you, who have no time, while he has so much!

And this is his laughter, too, like hope, but not laughter any
    more, just a smile,
a smile no longer childish,
even though coming from a faithful heart,
he isn't defending himself, despite being humiliated
by having to sell his father's hat and ring—
it's the bitter smile of a man, steep as the stakes
in a game played by poetry and a madman in the presence of
    life and death—
it's the wrinkled face of a man who knows
that even God, soon enough, was sorry to have created
    man . . .

There is nothing without pain.
Even a vineyard *bears* wine.

The road from Walktown to Wingtown is hard . . .
Let me tell you a short story ad excelsa:

It was around St. Anne's Day, when water is in bloom,
it was raining and chilly. I was tired
and hungry . . . Quartz pebbles underfoot and woods on
    the horizon
made me hope I'd find a glassworks soon.
I did, I got warm, I got some food and sleep.
As I was leaving, I met a woman at the door,
wiping tears on her apron; she told me not to go through
    the woods.
But there was no other way to go and I went forward
without asking her why . . . I was soon to know.
After walking for an hour I realized I was all alone,
I hadn't scared away a woodpecker, doe, or
    light-footed weasel,
but I was surrounded by a blind rustling sound that
chilled my spine, a rustling of thousands of tiny wings,
    a rustling
that stopped dead whenever I stopped . . . Then I saw
the whirling immobility one knows from paintings on
    columns . . .
The painting was black and white . . . As soon as I moved,
there was the rustling again, the anxiety, and again
that murky dimness making me use my eyes like torches.
Suddenly I was in past ages and I felt

the skull of weak memory, memory that by sundown
was to give back to me the awareness that I'd gotten lost and
    it was nun moths
making the woods shiver and making me shudder.
And then I smelled the villainous instinct . . . I don't like
the scent of lilac. I always thought that her sleeve at the bar
was filled by the arm of a night guard watching over the
    deceased body of all flowers . . .
And indeed, I could feel it,
that intrusive smell of decay wanting to be inhaled by a
    noseless man.
And besides, there was a senility that seemed forever
    rejuvenated—
and all the quivering moments of those moths
(the rustling increased with the humidity of the air after
    yesterday's rain!)
changed into an endless duration . . .
And it wanted death, not only the death of a tree, but
    yours too,
and it struck your face with the pliability
of a cube, if it were rounded . . .
How it echoed! How alone I was!
If I at least had a love letter in my pocket!
If I at least walked a horse by the rein! If there were
at least a bear's ear or a squirrel's little ear
or the spittle of a hunted deer,
or a woodpecker; a woodpecker doesn't mind its nose . . .
But never mind, never mind! Only the rustling, rising
into a wailing wind in the crematorium's chimney.

Once I saw a bee-shed burning. The fire was set by someone
who could never be proved guilty, because human evil
is secret . . . That day in the woods,
where magic was done, I could feel obvious evil,
the nun moths were wallowing in that evil,
they struck my face, spat in it, they excreted, mated,
stank, rustled, there were millions of them,
no one, not even God, would have destroyed them,
not even by a spark from the flint stone of omnipotence,
so self-assured, beguiling, and cunning they were,
spurning even the devil, their begetter,
they created themselves for themselves, and to make soulless
means to murder . . .

Unguarded against such spite,
I felt I'd die soon, I'd loved too little—
I felt those nun moths had (even though inverted)
what I never had: patience . . .
I also realized that though we still had
some woods and groves, there was no longer any
    virgin forest . . .
And now the woods will die, too, because promises
    were turned
into a merciless contract . . . And ever since then I often
ask whether I'd like to live again . . .

Poetic glory always speaks in the third person,
because it has only a simile to pit against God's measure . . .
A poet is a seer of the present, and that is why Quevedo
predicted the fate of the Spanish colonies,

it was Seneca who prophesied the discovery of America,
Chlebnikov foretold the year of the Russian revolution,
but Virgil saw the birth of Christ forty years beforehand . . .

A poet's every wish comes true,
none of his wishes can come true!
Every book, an unfinished book,
as if you said: behold the future,
because it's a book for the library of paupers.

And if every saint and every priest is Simon of Cyrene
(because he helps Christ carry the cross),
no matter how challenging this comparison may be:
a poet's violent heart
beats mainly in little stories,
his compassion pays in bloody sweat
for every cheap fate,
and when the soul
is called by the simplest of things,
he's beside them already, with them, *loyal*,
he affirms their mystery by his vision,
knowledge of events means nothing to him,
science, that cow on stilts, means nothing—
if knowledge matters, then it's knowledge of the heart,
he'll exchange large canvases of history
for a loft window,
opened perhaps into the Mycenaean layers of Troy,
Ben Jonson watched the battle of the Carthaginians against
    the Romans
on his big toe—

as for me, in those Mycenaean layers,
I was touched and moved to tears
by dust spilled into dust,
and in the dust a rattle made from a bone,
meant for a baby, a girl no doubt,
because I favor little girls,
it was the smallest rattle in the world,
O for a little girl, I saw her,
I saw her, alone, a little one alone,
in her cradle, and her little left hand and on that left hand
one little nail, illuminated by the kitchen fire,
a real fire, giving warmth by fleeing,
she was a little one alone,
so tiny and scrawny, as if fed on crickets' notes,
but her eyes were so melancholy and penetrating
that a poet, simply because of the enormity of his love,
can only see through tears in this world . . .

It wasn't easy, later,
to get the smallest ring in the world
for that girl. But they got it,
and a pocket Bible for the groom . . .
I was sorry it was raining at their wedding.*
Their carriage passed a wall behind which the knacker
was skinning a carcass . . . The wedding horses, with eyes of
    blind worms
and nostrils opened by the earthly key,

*Translators' note: Rain was a good omen at a Czech wedding. People would say:
"Good luck rained for them."

trembled and spooked . . . They had to be whipped
and led by the reins . . . The road ran
through a poppy field and later through a ravine that
forced a streamlike bend in the river . . . But before
reaching the church, the clapper of the bell broke loose . . .
A bad omen! But they were married by force . . .
They were told: If fate wants you to . . .

A poet who doesn't know himself, who doesn't know much
    about passion,
can only fall silent now,
because he thinks fatalism is too irresponsible,
because at the first disappointment he might make excuses
about fate, chance, resignation, apathy . . .

And you, laughter, joy, misery, and song—
where are you then? . . . If it's on Good Friday
that people believe treasures are revealed and ghosts dry
    their money,
on the ninth day despair is like nine stones . . .
On a day like that (and it can be made to last for years)
even time, once having taken refuge in the poem written at
    the time,
wants now, so soon, the death of the poem,
and the poet has nothing the eye could bear . . .
And it's at that time that his neighbors let him, of all people,
be dragged by lice into a print left by a horse's hoof . . . The
    wind stopped, too . . .

Will you, God, have mercy on him,
so that he holds on and doesn't take his life?

from Deathly Ill: 1961-1965

Certainly

—We walked around the lake two times
and didn't find it.
—Did you walk on dry sand?
—Yes!
—Where did you faint?
—In the place where you left it.
—And then?
—As you can see, here we are, totally bewildered.
—Yes, with nothing!
—Is that a reproach?
—No! But since you don't know what it's about,
you have to go back! You'll certainly find it!

Bitterly

You haven't been here in a long time,
so it's no use testing
whether the door still creaks,
and it's no good seeing
that the beautiful elm has been cut down,
and it's no good seeing the wrinkled wall
marked by arteries of the heartless ivy—
and it's no use entering this dilapidated house,
where the cellar and ceiling once
resonated with laughter . . .

For the bitterly convincing awareness that you're alive,
you don't need the dead . . .

Again?

So once again, night, you're in collusion with nature,
and once again you're questioning me?
All right then, I loved life,
and that's why I sang about death so often.
Without death, life is impossible to feel,
with it, life is just thinkable,
and therefore absurd . . .

Here and There

for Josef Sima

One hardly dares to admit
that we got so merry
on just wine, praising gods,
those without pain . . .
Because this is what we felt:
that the world is walking right through us
and we can stop it here and there . . .

Then who would have thought
that for this reason death
would have children with children!

Autumn

The tree still has a few leaves
but is not clothed in them any more,
because it wants to talk
to a more mysterious world
where it will be alone,
even though incognito perhaps . . .
And the statue under the tree,
fed by the fat of its haunches,
doesn't know what to think of the future
when it distrusts the heart . . .

And children? Children don't want an apple,
they want a *bigger* apple . . .
And Adam? He had the chance to be immortal
only once, but he dies all the time . . .

Mother

Mother, I still miss you,
and I miss you where it hurts most!

Tear, are you the same as you were in my youth,
or do you grow old too, with an aging man?

Knowledge isn't vision. But it's repeated.
That's one of the reasons we die . . .

from A Rooster for Aesculapius:
1966-1967

Evening

We tossed the astronomical atlas
bound in Copernicus's skin into the fireplace
to warm you.
You curled up, glittering, in the showering sparks
and dancing shadows, and you destroyed
any allegory, the dead mother
of the dead ornament, decoration, stylization.
Then you fell asleep. Under the skirt too.

In such silence,
what was said in a hermitage
should only be heard in a whorehouse . . .

Nasci, Pati, Mori . . .

What might this autumn,
maybe my last one, want? What might
this wind want, breaking the branches
filled with fruit like a trespasser,
as if to have it over and done with
before the fall of the last sweet?
What might this storm want, if the point
is just the burned rags of dead clouds
without diminution and nothing more?

Your life is helplessly silent,
lost in the heart, never found in love . . .

In October

And how about the storm that time in October?
Do you remember? The entire oak grove
was destroyed and the fish
in the lake perished. The vineyard
that would have yielded ten seven-pail barrels
was ravaged. Darkness beat
its antlike chest. Thunderbolts
traced the signature of Aeschylus.
Words emptied of meaning
were not big enough to be held,
so they retreated, retreated into themselves.

A good time for adultery . . .

Orchard

What silence, what sorrow,
what crying, what solace
made you wander after all these years
into the orchard, where once
the mad girl screamed and swore,
and tore her clothes from her body and from her clothes,
and bled as virginity bleeds
from hunger and womanhood from satiety,
but she was unable to cry . . .

Today, almost falteringly and shyly
and very gently the breeze lifts leaves
and watches the fruit that
wants to stay hidden
without being overlooked . . .

Only Death

The ancient terror, the ancient dread—
and it has a child's face . . . It's because
in our imagination
we never admit it, because
mother is with us. And it's she
who keeps asking: "Are you feeling better now?"

Only death asks no questions . . . Alone . . .
Art for art's sake . . .

from Second to Last: 1968-1971

At the Feast

I don't think it'll be a cloudburst,
but stay, because it will rain.
And although it's getting dark, one can still
see the books of clouds
burned by the hangman of the setting sun,
one can still see the orchard,
the bushel of apples, the window frames,
and the words, confessed and kept like a secret.
Is it an illusion or a fantasy
when one worries about everything corporeal?

There are more dead than the dead . . .

Like Children

The presence of a woman! At any time? O no!
Things experienced together can be
love that goes against love.
Only in pain do we become like children:
we look for mother. What a child:
knows nothing and cries already!
We know nothing either, but we cry
later . . .

And There

"Look!" he said, "a plague cemetery,
and it's bigger than Denmark!" Some trees
have a reason to softly ascend
the contents of the lower hill. Remote
and somehow innocently overlooked,
tiny squares of spindle trees mate
with wild hops. The wall
hasn't missed anything that might separate it
from the girl tending geese in the stubble field.
And there, at the wall, he lies
and waits to be alone at last,
the pre-Hamlet Shakespeare
of the post-Shakespeare Hamlet . . .

Mothers after the War

for Jaroslav Seifert

There are many who court God.
There are many who curse.
There are many who won't forgive.
There are many who help themselves
by blaming destiny, although they've never
gotten to know it very well . . . There are many
who have gone mad . . . But there isn't
a single one who would
re-enter her life . . .

Scattering grain to pigeons,
one of them harshly told you:
"I know my boy's been
dead a long time, but
he still doesn't answer my letters . . ."

from Good-bye?: 1972-1977

Never I

You got along with animals,
except for one German shepherd.
You got along with reptiles,
except for one snake.
You got along with birds,
except for one blue tit.
You got along with things
as sincere as
the creaking of doors in Mozart's apartment.
You often got along with a man,
but never with people, never with people
who without mercy
forced you to give up the world
in the children's playground . . .

The Test

Subjected to long torture
by hunger and thirst, he confessed
even his hidden tears. He was allowed
to drink one. Did he drink it? Yes . . .
Then he was given bird seed.
Did he eat it? Yes . . . Then
he was brought flesh from an executed
fellow prisoner. Did he eat it? Yes, he did . . .
One realizes with dread and shame
that this happens all the time
until it falls into senile oblivion.
This is a very chilly place . . .

Letter I

—You're dying . . . Did you enjoy life? . . .
—Yes!
—Why?
—Once under an old plane tree
a girl I didn't know handed me a letter
and went away . . .
—Did you read it?
—Yes.
—What did it say?
—Nothing!

A Triptych from 1975

I.

Oh Welt, ich muss dich lassen, sang Brahms,
and it's true: we've been so threatened
all the time, as if our Guardian Angel
needed a Guardian Angel
of his own . . . Now both of them are leaving,
and inside yourself you
are barely memory . . . And you wanted to defend yourself?

II.

You feel as if you don't exist
and on top of that somehow
don't want to exist . . .

But who knows if in a moment like that you're not
yourself . . .

III.

You have nothing more to say,
silence has turned away from you,
and death itself has disowned you.

Letter II

When roses have stopped spitting blood
and have closed their mouths in the last buds,
and when consumptive stinging nettles
make friends with burdock,
I'll be happy to welcome you
in the garden I don't possess.

I'll be happy to kiss both your hands,
I'll be happy to offer you wine in the arbor,
but it'll be behind a hawthorn fence
that I don't possess either.

And I'm writing this to you as *nobody*,
who loved you,
because I don't exist any more . . .

Forever

I feel no hunger,
so I'll make it!
says everybody from murderers
to conquerors . . .

Despite ruins, the desert, and no people,
it's true that there still is
spring, summer, autumn, and winter.

Orpheus

He couldn't read, write, count,
but he sang. When he died,
women washed his body
with a sponge. When
they touched his genitals,
he began to sing . . . In terror
they fled and spread
the news . . .
He died unburied . . .

Wesleyan Poetry in Translation

Translated from the Czech
Mirroring by Vladimír Holan

Translated from the French
The Book of Questions (7 works in 4 volumes)
  by Edmond Jabès
Fables from Old French translated by
  Norman Shapiro

Translated from the Italian
The Coldest Year of Grace by Giovanni Raboni

Translated from the Lithuanian
Chimeras in the Tower by Henrikas Radauskas

Translated from the Portuguese
An Anthology of Twentieth-Century Brazilian Poetry
  edited by Emanuel Brasil and
  William Jay Smith
Brazilian Poetry 1950–1980 edited by
  Elizabeth Bishop and William Jay Smith

Translated from the Spanish
Off the Map by Gloria Fuertes
Times Alone by Antonio Machado
With Walker in Nicaragua by Ernesto Cardenal

About the Author

Vladimír Holan was born in 1905. He worked in a Czechoslovakian government pension office from 1927 to 1933 and edited two arts journals from 1933 to 1940. He began to write poetry full-time in 1940. During the Second World War he lived on a small pension and what little he could make from his writing. In 1948 he was accused of "decadent formalism" and his work was officially ignored until 1963. In 1964 he received the Award of the Union of Czechoslovak Writers and in 1968 the country's highest artistic award when he was named National Artist and Laureate of the State. He died in 1980, leaving a canon of more than 3000 pages in ten volumes.

About the Translators

C. G. Hanzlicek's first book of poetry, *Stars*, won the 1977 Devins Award. He has published three other books of poetry, most recently *Calling the Dead*, and received a fellowship from the National Endowment for the Arts in 1976. He lives in Fresno, where he is professor of English at California State University, Fresno.

Dana Hábová is a free-lance translator who lives and works in Prague. She has translated two books, *Sagittal Section* (with Stuart Friebert) and *Interferon, or On Theater* (with David Young), written by Miroslav Holub, a Czech poet. She has also translated natural history books from Czech into English, and specializes in simultaneous translations for film voice-overs.

About the Book

Mirroring has been composed in Sabon by G & S Typesetters of Austin, Texas. It was printed on 60 lb. Glatfelter B-31 and bound by McNaughton & Gunn Lithographers of Ann Arbor, Michigan. Design by Joyce Kachergis Book Design and Production, Inc. of Bynum, North Carolina.
Wesleyan University Press, 1985.